OBSESSED WITH

BASS

AARON NEMEC

THE ESSENTIAL HISTORY OF

MIAMI BASS

1985 - 1993

INTRODUCTION

Around 2010, while in grad school for art at Purdue University in Indiana, I was doing a lot of projects about music culture. Something led me to think about bass and wonder why it was everyday I would hear various cars booming around town. The local sports talk radio station also had the low frequency levels set uncomfortably high in their mix for some reason. I thought about how when I was a teen in the 1990s nearly every boombox had a button that could automatically increase the bass. Want to let the whole world know how awesome your music is??? You don't just turn up the volume, you gotta crank the bass too! There was something about bass that made it desirable. All this led me to write a brief essay titled *Why Bass?* in which I attempted to understand the popularity of bass through cultural trends, technological advances, and the physiological effects of sound. While doing all this research I also got heavily into the history of the bass music genre, particularly Miami bass. I scoured Discogs for record covers and credits. The material I ran into from the 1980s and 90s displayed a distinct and bizarre regional DIY aesthetic to the culture that piqued my curiosity. There were tons of DJs and producers collaborating. The cover art had weird drawings of futuristic spaceships, racks of speakers, funky customized cars and trucks, and a lot of sexualized, offensive depictions of women. Everything visual was very cartoonish and awkward. I read about DJs throwing together quick mixes to play at clubs and trying to get the hot single pressed before the next big one dropped. The multiple stories the material pulled me towards was confusing, mysterious, and electric. There was something to unwrap from the formulaic trashiness combined with a pompous facade, like Las Vegas and Disneyland. I became obsessed with trying to understand bass.

I spent the next eight years going back to the topic. I compiled links to stories, emailed people, and studied album credits. The album art was what first grabbed my attention, so I envisioned telling the story of Miami bass through a book that cataloged the cover art. Well, it became evident that the story I wanted to tell went beyond the artwork and the scope of the entire project was too large. It needed serious editing if it were to serve any purpose. So instead of being comprehensive, I decided to only address some major figures and ideas of Miami bass through publishing this zine, while providing some imagery. Anyone can dig deeper for more information or better image quality.

Until I began this research my exposure to bass music was very limited. Years ago, while I was working at a CD store in a small Michigan town in the late 1990s, there was one repeat customer who would always special order bass music. The guy was muscular, like a tank. He wore his hair in a tall, crisp flat-top that was shaved around the sides and back. He would ride a mountain bike that was too small for him to this stripmall music store. Anyway, he would special order these bass CDs and then get huffy at how much they cost once they came in, leave them, and ride away. He never bought one, so over time he had built-up a nice little stack of bass music that we eventually had to just put out on the floor. The one album he ordered that I clearly remember was titled *Booty Bass* and had a pair of shiny butts on the cover framed by a

black and white checkerboard pattern. I never listened to that CD, but the blatancy of the cover and the mystique of this basshead character has stuck with me over time. Now that I have listened to a lot of older Miami Bass, I can't really say that I am interested in it for the music. Not that I dislike it, but my perspective comes solely as a total outsider still trying to understand the culture. I wonder where that bass guy is these days and wish I had gotten his input on the subject when I had the chance to.

One theory I have to explain the potent strangeness of the genre is that the geography of Florida, and Miami in particular, helped nurture bass music culture. Maybe being physically isolated at the end of a peninsula apart from the rest of the continental United States helped concentrate the scene as it grew. It must feel wrong to have experienced it firsthand as a local and see bass become so widely popular, only to then see the Miami bass genre remain ignored by larger music institutions as a whole. Maybe it was never taken seriously. Maybe it is the kind of music that doesn't want to be taken seriously. The Ramones and Sex Pistols were certainly cartoonish and goofy in nature, but they are historically celebrated without question as part of the emergence of punk. Maybe the difference is that punk fit neatly into the arc of rock music. The themes and styles it embraced elevated a genre it was naturally grown out of. A lot of Miami bass music was focused on the sound instead of the song. It branched more directly into car audio bass, but also has had some influence on hip hop. I would argue that the recognizable (to the point of formulaic) aesthetics of punk and Miami bass are equally referenced in contemporary popular music trends. And decades later there are still purists among both punk and bass genres. So what makes music *good* music? What makes music worthy of critical celebration? What makes music important?

Trying to clarify the contributions of everyone from the formative days of Miami bass is an exhausting task. New stuff was being churned out regularly and the creative work behind a hit song or hot group may not be conclusive despite the names that are credited. Verifying information can be problematic since aliases were often used and various contributors might have rotated behind a single group name. The credentials and details in this book have been selected from what is known about releases from their packaging and labels combined with portions of past interviews and personal email correspondences in an effort to highlight stories and connections between artists. There is also this bass historian, PappaWheelie Joe, who throughout the early 2000s was working on a Miami bass history project. There is a now-defunct Yahoo Groups forum Joe initiated to post some stories he had heard or found and people who were part of the scene would contribute in reply. There's so much riff-raff in the details and posturing that I can't imagine anyone successfully putting the entire history together in a coherent, credible fashion. So I want to give PappaWheelie Joe proper acknowledgement for what comes from his work moderating that forum. He also claims to have recorded the first version of "*Who Let The Dogs Out*" in 1992 and to have passed on an opportunity to be the vocalist for Limp Bizkit,[1] both of which are entirely possible. I dunno. What is clear is that the origin and growth of Miami bass, like most region-based music genres, does not start at one specific date or person. The region itself is the unifying factor. I have this vision that one day, as sea levels rise, Miami will become a lost city submerged somewhere off the coast. Bass music is a part of that city's culture and history that has rippled across the entire globe. I guess this book is a way for me to feel like I am helping preserve and make sense of where those ripples originated from.

Thanks for reading.

Aaron Nemec
defmess.com
February 2019

1 statemaster.com/encyclopedia/PappaWheelie (accessed February 25, 2019)

AMOS LARKINS II

The one figure who emerges as the most prominent in molding the sound of bass music is Amos Larkins II. His father worked for TK Records, a Miami disco mainstay founded by music mogul Henry Stone. Amos was a trained jazz musician that started recording as a session musician for the label when he was a teenager. He soon began producing electro tracks for Sunnyview Records which had formed from the remnants of TK Records as disco was fading out.[2] Amos was influenced by the local electro music that was utilizing the Roland TR-808 drum machine. This included Pretty Tony Butler, who was producing and releasing freestyle and electro under his own Music Specialist label, and a 1983 electro release by Osé titled *"Computer Funk"*, which was an early production by James McCauley.[3] The distinctive heavy bass drum of the TR-808 would define it as a signature instrument for the Miami bass sound.

Amos, now armed with a TR-808 and the full Sunnyview recording studio, was hired by Henry Stone to produce and release three to five electro records per week.[4] These were often put out on smaller labels (Nezz, Prime Choice, On Records) as trials before getting larger distribution through Sunnyview.[5] Amos

2 miaminewtimes.com/music/amos-larkins-ii-on-learning-the-music-biz-by-breaking-into-tk-records-studio-6473885 (accessed February 20, 2019)
3 daily.redbullmusicacademy.com/2015/10/amos-larkins-interview (accessed February 21, 2019)
4 daily.redbullmusicacademy.com/2015/10/amos-larkins-interview (accessed February 21, 2019)
5 miaminewtimes.com/music/amos-larkins-ii-on-miami-bass-ghetto-jump-and-who-left-lukes-

would attend weekly shows and talk to scenemakers like Luther Campbell, known as Luke, about what trends were hot in order to come up with ideas for new records. Back in the mid-1980s, Luke and the Ghetto Style DJs would perform in dance halls and skating rinks around Miami, in Liberty City and Carol City venues like the Pac Jam, Studio 183, and Super Star Roller Tech.

Luke recalls: "[The Ghetto Style DJs] would do the call and response and chants, but, at the same time, we were making up dances. Every week, it would be something different. The first dance was the first rap record [in Miami], *'Ghetto Jump.'* I used to put this Wild West theme song on and say, 'Everybody Ghetto Jump,' and I'd have 2,000 people in the skating rink jump up at the same time, and

name-off-the-sunnyview-label-6463884 (accessed February 21, 2019) do crazy stuff in the air. These guys [Krush II] came and said, 'We want to do a record.'"[6]

Amos' memory of the event is similar to Luke's: "So one night I was at the Super Star Roller Tech skating rink and I saw these people doing this crazy ass dance...That same night, I went over to the Pac Jam where Luke was playin', and the people were doing the same dance. So I asked Luke, 'What the fuck is that?' and Luke said, 'That's the Ghetto Jump, and you should do a record on it.' He said to me, 'If you do a record on that dance, it's gon' blow up.' Well hell, you ain't gotta beat me over the head with a pogo stick. So I went straight to the studio immediately."[7]

Amos is credited as producer under the alias of "T. Green" on the first release for *"Ghetto Jump"* under the Nezz label. Luke's contributions are denoted by the phrase "Created by The Wild And Crazy Luke Skywalker". After the first release sold so well, subsequent releases through Sunnyview would list Amos by name and remove any mention of Luke. This slight and lack of royalties may have inspired Luke enough to produce and release his own material through Luke Skyywalker Records[8], which quickly became a recognized label and Luke one of the most well-known artists to originate from the Miami bass scene because of censorship battles as part of the rap group 2 Live Crew. I don't want to delve into the 2 Live Crew story, since it has been well-documented. I do want to point out the cool Luke Skyywalker logo and

6 daily.redbullmusicacademy.com/2015/10/nightclubbing-the-pac-jam (accessed February 21, 2019)

7 miaminewtimes.com/music/amos-larkins-ii-on-miami-bass-ghetto-jump-and-who-left-lukes-name-off-the-sunnyview-label-6463884 (accessed February 21, 2019)

8 "Who's Who: Luke Skyywalker Records", *New On The Charts*, Vol 14. No 2, February 1989

that there are several albums with cover art and lettering done by Manny Morell, who did a lot of album art for various Miami bass releases. George Lucas won a lawsuit against Campbell in 1990, so the label name was eventually shortened to just Luke Records.[9]

One of the early hits produced by Amos was the very first recording to have the bass ultra-heavy in the mix. It happened accidentally. Late one night in 1985, as Amos was mixing the track *"Commin' In Fresh"* by Double Duce he was also partying in the studio with a stripper. He got distracted enough during the session that by the time he submitted the track for mastering he did not have time to review the levels. It was sent out to be pressed and released to stores the following week. "That Friday, I happened to be in a flea market...I'll never forget walking in the store and my friend the record store owner putting on *'Commin' in Fresh.'* ...when I heard that over-compressed bass not only was it too long, but it was tearing up the fuckin' speakers. That's when I said to myself, 'Oh, shit, I did a major fuck-up. I didn't check the bass. Henry Stone is gonna execute me.' I mean, it was humming like bass from hell, so I looked around the store to all the people and the strangest

9 Philips, Chuck (September 26, 1990) "Campbell Pays $300,000 in Skyywalker Settlement" *Los Angeles Times*

thing happened. Everybody looked up asking, 'Who the fuck is that?' and 'What's the name of that record?' People got in line asking for a copy right there. I was puzzled…And unbeknown to me, my buddy who owned that same mixtape record store had already put it on cassette on some of his new mixes, and as I was coming out of the flea market, a car passed by and it had my song on, *'Commin in Fresh'* and the shit was literally tearing up the fuckin speakers in the car. As they passed by me, I waved them down…and I asked them, 'Do y'all like that sound? Y'all like that shit?' And they said, 'Hell yeah, that bass is the shit.' I was fuckin' in a daze."

"So I went straight back to the studio told Henry about my fuck-up on the mix, but that I thought it was a good fuck-up and that I think we are onto something and that he had to pull that record and let me tighten up the sound a little with levels. From that point on, I just started perfecting the bass sound on future records, and that's how Miami bass was born…It was a mistake, and once I saw that people were into it, I did more records like it."[10] Amos is credited under another alias, Leon Green, on the label for *"Commin in Fresh"*. As he produced more and more of these bass records, Amos states, "nobody was

10 miaminewtimes.com/music/amos-larkins-ii-on-his-miami-bass-sound-all-a-mistake-caused-by-cocaine-and-a-stripper-6450084 (accessed February 24, 2019)

calling it bass music, nobody was calling it nothing. We were calling it drop. 'Oh, that track got that drop.' Block parties and skating rinks were popular for a long time, and they were calling it drop." As Amos's reputation grew, he was chosen by teenage Adrian Hines to be producer when his father—and 4-Sight Records owner, Billy Hines— let Adrian put a record out on his label. Adrian had a concept for a song titled *"Bass Rock Express"* and his father wanted the track to be built around a sample from the theme song to *Green Acres*, so Amos took it from there. Amos recalls, "If you listen to *'Bass Rock Express'* really closely, you hear my voice. It was not Adrian, it was me. He couldn't do it...I said, 'Billy, this going to take all night... Let me go in there, show him how to do it, and from that point on he will know what to do.' I said, 'Give me the words, let me do it, then you'll know how to do it.' [Adrian] didn't know how to pronounce that shit like that. I said, 'Fuck, that ain't going to do it.' So I showed him how to accentuate and exaggerate his words and do it."[11] Released in 1985, the record was the first for MC A.D.E. (Adrian Does Everything), and was the first appearance of "bass" by name and theme in addition to sound. Adrian did go on to write and record several of his own productions. Amos is once again credited as Leon Green.

11 daily.redbullmusicacademy.com/2015/10/amos-larkins-interview (accessed February 24, 2019)

JAMES McCAULEY

A dominant character within the beginnings of Miami bass is James McCauley, a producer and arranger from Ft. Lauderdale, just north of Miami. In addition to the previously mentioned Osé record that inspired Amos Larkins II, James also produced many of his own electro records in the early to mid 1980s. It was then under the monikers of Maggotron and DXJ ("DX" a nod to the Oberheim DX drum machine) that James began completely embracing bass as a concept in every aspect of his releases: in the sound, the words, the titles, the album artwork. Bass became a whole lifestyle and universe.

Nearly all of the Maggotron material is steeped in sci-fi and self-mythology. James placed bass at the forefront amongst a spacey, technological backdrop that paid homage to Afrika Bambaataa as well as the electro funk of George Clinton ("Maggot" Brain). There is often a metaphorical reference to a bass planet, and I cannot tell if that planet is supposed to be an imagined Earth dominated by the power of bass or another planet that bass originated from. There are also references to speaker monsters that are capable of destroying cities, ancient cultures that worshipped bass, etc. Several of the Maggotron albums are dense with text that humorously puns the foes of bass and contemporaries in the Miami bass scene and beyond. This orchestrated bass worship would also come to define the genre itself. If you say it, it will be so...

A 2001 article in the *New Miami Times*[12] chronicles a story from James in which a few fans from Germany tracked him down. It was 1997, at the dawn of the internet, when the fans found James' contact info by visiting the Pandisc label headquarters. Pandisc was run by Bo Crane, and somewhat became *the* label for all things bass. Bo was a major figure in the 70s disco scene as a DJ and publisher of the biweekly *Disco Report*. He hung out at TK Records a lot, just to have his finger on the pulse. Pandisc was his post-disco project and it failed to hold onto any identity till it signed James, who had been bouncing around several labels prior.[13] Pandisc ended-up releasing most of the Maggotron and DXJ related projects, and were a parent label for the ones through Jamarc and Jamron which I think James was running himself. The business reputation of Pandisc is dubious, as James

12 miaminewtimes.com/music/electro-mecca-6353409 (accessed February 25, 2019)

13 Schulman, Sandra (August 30, 1996) "'Disco King' is Still In Tune" *South Florida Sun-Sentinel*

has referred to them as "Paindisc" or "Scamdisc".[14] With some effort, he broke things off with them completely in the summer of 2000, calling them out as "blood-sucking thieves".[15]

When the two German fans found James via Pandisc they enthusiastically purchased as much as they could, especially from the Jamarc and Jamron labels. James had crates of his old stuff sitting around at home, and no idea that it was gaining collector's value from the growing popularity of early 80s electro in Europe. The mythological Maggotron was earning a reputation as a pioneer of Miami bass culture.

One of my first draws to Maggotron was the cover art on some of his earlier releases, which visualized the sci-fi bass worship of his music. Most of these were done by LaMar Johnson, signed neatly in the corner with LAMAR next to a little brush 'n' palette doodle. LaMar was a freshman that attended the same high school where James was a senior. James knew of LaMar's artwork through a couple of classes they had together. As James began his music project, he

14 groups.yahoo.com/neo/groups/Miami_Bass_History/conversations/topics/4391?guccounter=1 (accessed February 25, 2019)

15 miaminewtimes.com/music/electro-mecca-6353409 (accessed February 25, 2019)

would approach LaMar with concepts for the artwork and LaMar would execute the idea. Perhaps the most well-known Maggotron project is *The Bass That Ate Miami* which has a LaMar cover featuring a giant, city-destroying speaker monster. The character was LaMar's idea and makes several cameos as part of the dense Maggotron lexicon of imagery and language.[16] The bass worshipping and other-worldly qualities James brought to Miami bass championed the genre as a futuristic, technological innovation. From there it branched into popular sub-genres. The booty bass genre combined it with raunchy sexualized themes and women's asses. Techno bass centered it around audio systems and car audio competition that was only concerned with achieving the lowest low frequencies. Grandiose speaker systems and slick, chromey automobiles. Neil Case, fellow Pandisc artist and innovator of techno bass, described it by noting, "car audio bass is about listening to sounds, not music."[17]

16 personal email from LaMar Johnson to the author (August 20, 2015)
17 electronicbeats.net/miami-with-bass-mekanik/ (accessed March 13, 2019)

CALVIN MILLS II

There is one 1989 James McCauley compilation project he titled *Miami Bass Machine* with LaMar Johnson artwork that depicts a scorpion spaceship destroying another spaceship as a horrified space traveler looks on and a space station blows-up in the distance. The original spaceship being destroyed is from the album *Rock This Planet* by Bass Patrol (artwork by Manny Morell) released on Joey Boy records in 1988. It was a friendly shot at the label, who James thought was attempting to imitate his style.[18] Calvin Mills II and his brother Carlton were the brains behind Bass Patrol, and some of the primary creative within the Joey Boy catalog. They had previously befriended James at the finals for a local radio station song contest in 1986, so this cover dis was nothing personal towards them.[19]

Calvin Mills II has his name all over the early Miami bass scene. Before doing production work at Joey Boy, he got his professional start with Pretty Tony on several early Music Specialist electro records, like *"Summer Delight,"* from 1983, on which Pretty Tony states Calvin "co-wrote and contributed greatly to the instrumentation."[20] In addition to Bass Patrol, Calvin had a hand in many projects once he signed with Joey Boy. He and Carlton fronted the R&B duo Rock Force. He did production, writing,

18 b-bartsbasscovers.blogspot.com/2013/08/cover-wars-part-6-bass-patrol-vs-miami.html (accessed February 26, 2019)
19 facebook.com/pg/Maggotron-62386418059/posts/ from June 7, 2018 (access February 27, 2019)
20 personal email from Tony Butler to the author (August 18, 2015)

and arrangements for rap groups such as The Miami Boyz and The M-4Sers, which comprised of his sister Fresh Celeste, his brother Slick V, and cousin Big Mouth T.[21] Fresh Celeste also recorded solo material through Joey Boy. Some of the more notable associations Calvin had at Joey Boy were centered around Disco Rick and The Dogs. Early on, Ricky Taylor got his Disco Rick nickname from Pretty Tony when he was a teenager in the Party Down DJs crew. They performed at skating rinks in the early 1980s, much like Luke and the Ghetto Style DJs that Amos Larkins connected with. Disco Rick closely followed Luke's instincts on style and trends.

"He didn't show me, I just watched. I didn't watch nobody else." He eventually hooked onto Hot Productions, another label founded by Henry Stone, and formed Gucci Crew. After a few albums, Disco Rick left the group over creative differences.

He had some ideas for new material, similar to what Luke was doing

21 personal email from Calvin Mills II to the author (March 21, 2019)

with 2 Live Crew, but, "more political and less about bitches."[22] So he latched on with Calvin at Joey Boy and formed The Dogs with three other guys, including Labrant "Ant D" Dennis. Their self-titled debut album released in 1990 peaked at #37 on the Top R&B/Hip-Hop Albums chart and included the group's most recognized song, *"Crack Rock"*, which featured a chorus of children taunting, "Yo' mama's on crack rock!" The cover depicts a scantily clad warrior woman riding a three-headed dog monster.

Disco Rick left the group by the third Dogs album, *K-9 Bass*. And as the group fizzled, Calvin began a new child rap group called The Puppies that essentially put the kids who provided vocals for the chorus of *"Crack Rock"* out front with cleaner material.[23] He hesitantly enlisted his own kids, Tamara Dee and Calvin III, to front the group. "I didn't really want them to be in the business because I knew how hard it could be.....I let them stay kids...It's not like I want to punish them with music."[24] Chaos Records, a subsidiary of Columbia, bought out The Puppies' contract from Joey Boy. Under the support of a major label, their song *"Funky Y-2-C"* sold over 280,000 copies and peaked at #40 in the Billboard Hot 100, #31 in the Hot R&B/Hip-Hop chart, and at #6 in the Billboard Hot Rap Singles charts. When success faded, the major label dropped the act. The elder Calvin fought to get naming rights for The Puppies back from Joey Boy, giving up a lot of money and ownership to over 60 songs.

Another part of The Dogs' aftermath story is centered around Labrant "Ant D" Dennis. Calvin was behind Labrant's 1993 solo album *Top Dog* by Ant D & The Puppies. Labrant

22 daily.redbullmusicacademy.com/2015/10/disco-rick-interview (accessed March 16, 2009)
23 mtv.com/news/2985787/moonlight-forgotten-frequencies/ (accessed March 23, 2019)
24 Piccoli, Sean (March 7, 1997). "Puppies Bounce Back With New Label, Album". *Sun-Sentinel.* Fort Lauderdale, Florida.

is currently serving a death sentence for the gruesome murders of Timwanika Lumpkins and Marlin Barnes in April of 1996. Both had been found badly beaten and barely alive in Marlin's dorm room at the University of Miami. They died a short-time later. It became a national story because Marlin was a linebacker for the Miami football team. His roommates and star teammates at the time were Earl Little and Ray Lewis. Each have spoken openly about the event. Earl was the one who discovered the victims early in the morning, there to pick up his car that Marlin had been borrowing. "When I opened the door, [Marlin] was lying on the floor. There was a pool of blood. I thought it was fruit punch. I thought he was playing a joke. I'm, like, 'Gosh, Marlin?' He tried to respond, but couldn't. I called his name again, and he turned his head. He had enough strength to turn his head and his face was all ... he didn't have a face at all. I mean, all his flesh was gone, crushed, whatever, just torn up." To remember Marlin, Ray keeps a collage he made from images of his friend that includes one photo of Labrant at the bottom. "A lot of people find it very weird, that I would put that picture up. I look at it and wonder what kind of heart a person has to have to hurt my friend. I mean, that wasn't just a quick bullet. Did he want to see him suffer?"[25]

Timwanika had been Labrant's girlfriend, and they had one child together. Their relationship was tenuous and violent. The couple had been living together, but

25 LeBatard, Dan (July 10, 2012). "Gone To Glory". *ESPN Magazine*. www.espn.com/espn/magazine/archives/news/story?page=magazine-19980504-article35 (accessed March 18, 2019)

according to Timwanika's brother, "she didn't want to see him, and he didn't know how to handle it."[26] She began dating Marlin, and a week prior to the murder Marlin had helped Timwanika move out. The night before being murdered, the two of them were seen kissing and hugging while attending an event at Club Salvation. They left to find Earl's car with the tires slashed. A tow truck gave them both a ride to Marlin's dorm around 6:00 am, and it was a few hours later that Earl first arrived.[27] In the wake of the murders, Disco Rick commented that Labrant "was the type to fall in love. He was a macho guy on the outside, but inside he had a heart. [Timwanika] is the girl he has loved for years."[28] Labrant claimed innocence in the days following the murders. His cousin testified to substantiate an apparent alibi. However, the evidence and witnesses against him were damning, and he was convicted and sentenced in February of 1999.

Calvin Mills II remained active throughout the 1990s and into the internet era. His importance to Miami bass, even if only by sheer volume, is often still overlooked. He currently has his own website at www.calvinmills.net and several videos posted to his YouTube channel for Convertible Records.[29]

---

26 si.com/vault/1996/04/22/212127/star-crossed-the-already-beleaguered-miami-football-program-must-now-deal-with-the-brutal-murder-of-a-player

27 floridasupremecourt.org/content/download/338625/3011928/07-2208_response.pdf (accessed March 19, 2019)

28 Pazdera, Donna and Benjamin, Jody (May 2, 1996). "Suspects Mother Reeling After Arrest, Says He Didn't Do It". *Sun-Sentinel*. Fort Lauderdale, Florida. (accessed March 18, 201) https://www.sun-sentinel.com/news/fl-xpm-1996-05-02-9605020029-story.html

29 youtube.com/user/ConvertibleRecords (accessed March 20, 2019)

THE BOOM

Miami bass seems to have peaked around 1988. A few words about some noteworthy people from that time:

Boot The Booty by MC Cool Rock & MC Chaszy Chess was the first recording to officially use the word "booty" in conjunction with Miami bass. The album was released in 1988 on Vision Records, a few years after much of the scene had become blatantly sexualized. Ironically this album cover does not contain any images of asses. MC Cool Rock was murdered[30] after this release, but some other contributors became key figures on their own. Beatmaster Clay D did the arranging and production work for the recordings, and DJ Magic Mike from Orlando contributed cuts and scratching. The two of them decided to

30 How this happened could not be verified. Personal email from DJ Magic Mike to the author states "I heard Ced had a hit out on him and they got him stopped at a railroad crossing" (March 21, 2019)

work on a new project as The Get Funky Crew with Prince Rahiem, a young friend Magic Mike had brought down from Orlando. Business dealings between Clay D and Vision were being done without Magic Mike, so he left and they removed his contributions. Prince Rahiem stayed behind.[31] Back in Orlando, Magic Mike co-founded his own label and his 1989 album *DJ Magic Mike and The Royal Posse* was certified platinum by 1994.[32]

L'Trimm stood out as a stylish hip-hop duo of two young women, Lady Tigra and Bunny D. They had signed with Henry Stone's Hot Productions, and had national success with their prophetic 1988 song *"Cars With The Boom."* They had

31 daily.redbullmusicacademy.com/2016/12/magic-mike-prince-rahiem (accessed March 21, 2019)
32 "DJ Magic Mike, Orlando's Rap Maestro Branching Out". *Orlando Sentinel*. Howard Greenberg. September 11, 1994. www.orlandosentinel.com/news/os-xpm-1994-09-11-9409070683-story.html (accessed March 21, 2019)

a falling out with Hot Productions when the label wanted to put co-writers in charge of re-shaping their sound. L'Trimm abandoned the recordings, and the label put out a dud using what was scrapped from the vocal sessions without the duo's input.[33]

Dynamix II was a project of Dave Noller. His breakthrough recording was *"Just Give The DJ A Break"*, which he took to Pandisc as a demo in 1987. James McCauley was in the office and told Bo Crane, "I can beat the snot out of that beat." So Pandisc passed,[34] and the track later became hugely successful after being reworked by reputable DJ **Eric Griffin** and released on his Bass Station Records.

In another example of the violence and tragedy that surrounds many of the Miami bass stories, Eric's early collaborator was Norberto Morales

33 Shapiro, Peter (2005) "L'Trimm", in *The Rough Guide to Hip-Hop*, Rough Guides
34 dissensus.com/showthread.php?t=3768&s=fdf7c1ae2b73052703bc3a0ce053c4b7 (accessed March 21, 2019)

who also owned the Bass Station club and was murdered in a drug deal. Eric continued to record with Missy Mist and other acts under his own label. According to Missy, Eric "kept a large entourage ever since Norberto's death in 1987. Norberto was killed in his home by someone he knew very well and allowed in. Eric feared he would face the same sort of tragic death." Sadly, he was killed in his hometown of East St. Louis in October of 1996 when he allowed a local group that he had been working with to come into his home. Once inside, they robbed Eric, beat him, and strangled him to death.[35] The 1990s were the long, strange wake of Miami bass. The sentiments and success of the tracks from L'Trimm and Dynamix II crystallized into

35 groups.yahoo.com/neo/groups/Miami_Bass_History/conversations/topics/4391?guccounter=1 (accessed March 21, 2019)

car audio bass. The whole decade of the 1990s is full of bass music albums and compilations made specifically for proving how powerful your car's system could be. They are often accompanied by odd early Photoshop cover art. The previously mentioned Neil Case was prolific during this time as Bass Mekanik and other monikers. Also noteworthy is the work from Power Supply, a car audio bass solo project of Derrick Rahming's who was member of the group Afro-Rican. They are known for their 1987 song *"Give It All You Got (Doggy Style),"* which was sampled in 2006 by Fergie in *"Fergalicious."* (side note: Derricks's own Hip Rock label has a 1993 album titled *Come Get Some* by the Get Some Crew. Its cover depicts perhaps the most offensive possible image of three men holding a gun to a woman's exposed butt.) The Neurodisc label, like Pandisc, was home to many anonymous compilations

of extreme bass with interchangeable artists and titles like *Sexual Bass*, *Dungeon of Bass*, and *Neurotic Bass*.

Car audio also included many Florida artists from beyond Miami like Techmaster P.E.B. from Sarasota and Quad Force from Tampa Bay. Many of these albums came with attached warnings of ULTRA LOW BASS that may damage the user's

equipment. I've tried listening to a few of these and the bass frequencies are so low they just disappear to silence. My PC speakers won't even try.

So here we are, nearly 35 years since Miami bass first began with Amos Larkins. Whether it is pure sound or part of a song, the brash machismo of a kickin' bass system is a universal symbol for power. A language all its own. If the city of Miami does disappear amongst rising sea levels, Miami bass will be a vital part of the city's cultural legacy. From the stew of cheap pastel aesthetics and deep tone worship we continually see in today's music to the dude cranking the bass to talk radio for that morning commute, Miami bass will live on.

Bass Erotica
Sexual Bass
BONUS: REVEALING PHOTOS OF BASS EROTICA INSIDE!
CAUTION: MEGA-LOW SEXUAL BASS. MAY DAMAGE SPEAKERS

BASS 305
VIRTUAL BASS
CAUTION
MEGA LOW BASS
May Damage Speakers
Produced by BASS 305

BASS DOMINATRIX
HARD BASS

GET SOME CREW
COME GET SOME
PARENTAL ADVISORY

DANNY D -N- DJ WIZ
BIGBUTTS&BASS

BASS TECH DXJ
BASS THE NATION

M.C. A.D.E.
IN THE ARMS OF

QUAD FORCE
FEEL THE REAL BASS
QUAD FORCE • FEEL THE REAL BASS
WARNING:
THE BASS LEVELS
IN THIS MUSIC MAY BE
HAZARDOUS TO YOUR SPEAKERS

QUAD QUEEN
QUEEN OF QUAD

MAX
KILLA
HERTZ

BASS SHOCK
WARNING
CONTAINS ELECTRO MAGNETIC
BASS WAVES MAY CAUSE
PERMANENT DAMAGE TO YOUR
SYSTEM ! ! !
Dungeon of Bass

BASS SYNDICATE
CYBERBASS–
VIRTUAL REALITY
Produced
& Engineered
by Bass 305
CAUTION
MEGA LOW BASS
May Damage Speakers

Microcosm's SCENE HISTORY series

Are you stoked about the history of your town? Do you find out interesting nuggets by talking to those who came before you or by scouting out details on Google and Wikipedia? Do you want a reason to hunt out some people you respect and fill in the gaps?

Well, the Scene History series is an opportunity to do just that. Like our Simple History Series, we will publish a paperback each year of the Scene History series that tell the story of a particular city's scene. (the series does not profile individuals, albums, or bands, but really must be framed around a real scene, no fiction!)

Suggested length is 15,000-30,000 words. Get as creative as you find gratifying. Learn about your favorite places and how things developed.

To pitch, just send a general summary of the scene that you are profiling, the years profiled, and your qualifications/interest to profile it! Will it be prose or comics? Do you have access to photos and images? Why are you excited to do this?

Submit or ask questions to joe@microcosmpublishing.com

$4.95 U.S. / $6.50 CANADA
ISBN 978-1-62106-480-0
9 781621 064800